John Pepper's ULSTER PHRASE BOOK

John Pepper's
ULSTER PHRASE BOOK

Illustrated by
Ralph Dobson

another Appletree haunbook

First published and printed by
The Appletree Press Ltd
7 James Street South
Belfast BT2 8DL
1982

British Library Cataloguing in Publication Data
Pepper, John
    John Pepper's Ulster phrase book.
    1. English language—Dialects—Northern Ireland
    I. Title
    427'.9416   PE2586

ISBN 0-86281-101-5

Contents

Foreword: 9

Map of *Norn Iron*: 10

Travel: 13

Hotels: 19

Eating and Drinking: 21

Shopping: 25

Entertainment: 29

Formal Occasions: 33

Sport: 35

Illness: 37

People: 41

Trades and Professions: 45

The Time and the Weather: 47

Numbers and Colours: 51

Survival Kits: 53

Dialogues Translated: 57

Test Your Word Power: 61

A *Morr Tung* Quiz: 63

Foreword

It is not a happy experience, when an introduction runs, 'This is Mrs Darthy Darty. Shizza frennafmine', to discover that the lady is actually Mrs Dorothy Doherty, that she is a friend of the speaker, and that her religion is not being indicated. The aim of this phrase book of Ulster's *morr tung* is to enable such situations to be delicately avoided, to offer a guide to its infinite variations, provide a de-coder for the uninformed, and to signpost the quicksands.

It is a vernacular with many rules and a wide variety of usages, a knowledge of which will keep the unwary out of trouble. Rules, for example, which turn the town of Omagh, in Co. Tyrone, into *Omer,* transform Bellaghy into *Blahey,* and result in Clogher becoming *Clawer.* It is also made clear that if you hear someone speak of *Nora Mean* that it is the speaker's way of finding out if you know what he is getting at. Similarly, if faced with the question 'Do you like fline?', this guide will make it clear that your knowledge of cuisine is not being explored, but that an effort is being made to find out if you feel at home in an aircraft, and that the statement 'Harran Woof—they built the Tonic' is a reference to the Belfast shipyard of Harland and Wolff, builders of the ill-fated *Titanic.*

In short, students of Ulster's *morr tung* will find here an outline of some of its strangest aspects, among them many which may well be a revelation to those who consider they speak it like a native. A familiar piece of guide book advice is that it is always best to avoid behaving like a tourist. This book is designed to help the tourist to avoid speaking like one.

Map of NORN IRON

By Air

Ulster people are compulsive talkers when on the move. Should you get into conversation on a flight to Northern Ireland is is useful to appreciate that the way you would put things is often at variance with the manner in which the natives often express themselves.

Fonda fline?

Are you a seasoned traveller?

Nathn bates a bitta crack. Wherrer ye fir?

I feel that conversation is pleasant on a journey. What is your destination?

13

Stime we tuk aff.	Aren't we rather late?
Cud ye truss that pilate?	Is the pilot experienced?
Spumpy, innit?	Isn't it somewhat rough?
Yunna baggage ture?	Are you on a package holiday?
Nowen we lite?	What time are we due to land?
Fits ruff it'll onny start me vamitin.	I hope we have a smooth flight otherwise . . .

By Sea

How d'ye ketch the Lirpool boat?	How far would I be from the Liverpool dock?
I'm steeritch. Do we get aff last?	I am travelling steerage. Where do I go?
I hope it's a nice crossin. Ave an awful wake stummick.	I trust it will be a pleasant voyage.
I hope the scringin doesn't keep me awake.	Is it a very noisy ship?
What kine affa tip is the stuart luckin?	What gratuity does the steward expect?
A'm goanta tho aff.	I am afraid I am about to be ill.

On Arrival

Ulster people always have a friendly greeting for the visitor on the tip of their tongue. It may not always sound like one and it is helpful to be aware of this.

Formawrite?	Is the form good?
Berrinup?	Are you bearing up?
Mannijin?	Are you managing all right?
Howlinawn?	Are you holding on?
Areye ritely?	How are you doing?
Kaipinfit?	Are you in good health?

14

By Car

When stopping at a garage the service you get can be influenced if you use the vernacular. In many cases this can win much greater respect.

Theea thee.	I would like three gallons of three-star petrol, please.
Shuvva quarta oil intil her. She gulps one down ivvery five mints.	Put in a quart of oil, please.
A gatta pumpture.	I have a flat type.
Givvos adrappa win.	I think the pressure needs checking.
Take a wee gawk at thoil.	Would you ensure that the oil is all right?
Ave gat spension barr.	Something seems to be amiss with the suspension.
Thowl thing's nivver outa th' garritch, so it issen.	The engine is giving me a lot of trouble.

Parking

Gawd I've stapt onna double yella. Wattle ado?	Are the authorities strict about double yellow lines?
Ken farren cars park in a yella zone?	Can I park in a parking zone?
Monea visitor. Mawlrite to putt it here?	I'm a stranger. Can I park here?
Mutch d'ye hafta pay inna street ye can't get out aff?	What are the regulations about driving in a cul-de-sac?
Am a buggered onna double yella?	I presume I'm in trouble if I park on a double yellow line?
If I park here wudda run the risk of getting been up?	I'm not sure if it is quite safe to park here. Would I be attacked?

15

By Taxi

Taxi drivers are less naturally inclined to take advantage of a visitor if they are addressed in their native tongue.

Tharches as quack as ye can.
Holywood Arches, and I'm in rather a hurry.

Harran Woof's.
The Harland and Wolff shipyard.

Amgoin past Galliker's.
I want to be dropped just past Gallaher's factory.

Tharts.
The Arts Theatre.

Take us up the Ormer.
About halfway along the Ormeau Road will do me.

Durm Street okay?
Durham Street, please.

Winser Pork.
I want Windsor Park.

Hard Street.
To Howard Street, please.

Belfast's black taxis often carry a number of passengers to different destinations in the same area, rather like a bus service. Passengers usually have plenty to say to each other.

Shappins sickinin.
Going round the shops has quite exhausted me.

I havta smooth masell.
I have a great deal of ironing to do when I get home.

Yizawl heddin down the Falls?
Are you going along the Falls Road?

I'l givvera good reddin out.
I'm going to speak bluntly to my sister-in-law.

Scriminall wather astin fer a perra tights.
The price of tights is really preposterous.

The wee lad hessa bittava sturr.
My small boy suffers from a slight speech impediment.

Snivverbeenaswarm.
I cannot remember such a stiflingly hot day.

16

By Bus

An ability to slip into the vernacular is also valuable when travelling by bus, ensuring that other passengers do not look on you as an oddity, and therefore someone faintly suspect.

Mucher ye luckin?	How much is the fare?
Thissus?	Is this where I get off?
Wennil we get there?	How long does the journey take?
Kenna get aff ni?	Can I alight here?
Am bina season.	I would like to purchase a season ticket.
Cud ye break a fiver?	Can you change a £5 note?

Asking the Way

Should you have to ask the way it should be borne in mind that local measurements can be haphazard. This is offered as a rough and ready guide to their variations.

It's just a wee while.	40-50 yards.
Ye cud be there before yer back.	200-300 yards.
Two shakes of a lamb's tail.	500 yards.
Soney a coupla spits down the road.	Less than half a mile.
Ach it's just a wee dander.	Slightly over half a mile.
Hardly a beagle's gowl away.	Three quarters of a mile.
If ye walk fast ye'll be there in half the time.	Upwards of a mile.
Sneer a mile.	Slightly less than a mile.
Sa ferr wee distance.	Up to five miles.

Sa quare lick, mind ye.	Up to ten miles.
Spout ten mints afore ye cum till McFadden's pub.	A twenty minute walk.
Slat farder than you'd think.	An hour's walk.

HOTELS

Hotels

Hotels in Northern Ireland generally offer excellent service, but it does no harm to indicate requirements in the manner of a native.

The hate's desprit sotis.   Our room is much too warm.

The wife's friz. Cud we have more clothes on the bed?   My wife is feeling the cold. We need more blankets.

Wud ye callus atate?   Could we be called at eight o'clock?

We need more tiles.	We could do with more towels.
Yer a bit mangey wi' the soap.	We need a few more bars of soap.
Shire's broke.	The shower doesn't seem to be working properly.
We cud do wi' a male.	We would like to have dinner?
Wennis brakefess?	What time is breakfast?
Stable's a dead loss.	We do not like this table.
What's the dammitch?	Could we have our bill, please?
Yew trian itton?	This bill is absurd.
We onny want a drappa tay.	All we require is a pot of tea.
Ware's the wumman's classit?	Could you direct me to the ladies' toilet?

Eating and DRINKING

Eating Out

Geeusafry.

I would like fried eggs and bacon, with fried bread.

That stew wuz the quare mark.

The stew was delicious.

Put some weeten on the plate.

Could we have brown bread as well as white?

Yir pirty oaten squaren fillin.

I am told your potato oaten bread has a good reputation.

Nathin bates a vision chips supper.

Fish and chips are very tasty.

A plaita tip's outa this world.	I am very fond of fried bread.
Spotted ern wud be just the job.	Would you have potted herring on the menu?
This dush's dirty.	This plate hasn't been properly cleaned.
Ouse about some city potatoes.	We would like some French fried potatoes.
Gettus the jeez boordan biskits.	Could we have the cheese board and biscuits?
Thaddick made me turn.	I found the haddock very poor.
Good plaita parritch puts hair on your chest.	Porridge for breakfast can be quite enjoyable.
The chile just sits there pickin.	My little girl has lost her appetite.
Gaeus yin a the oot yins.	I would prefer an egg from a free-range hen.
Gaeus baked necks.	We would like bacon and eggs.

In the Bar

Yew stannin?	If you like, you could buy me a drink.
Bias a wee jar/rosiner/quick wun.	Would you care to ask me to join you in a small Scotch?
Bias a battle by the neck.	I would like a bottle of beer.
A wudden say no till a chinnan tonick.	I'll have a gin and tonic, if I may.
Howl on man or I'll go home stovin.	I really shouldn't drink any more.
A'll hevta see what a pintapour wud do till me.	I shall try a pint of porter.
Luckat m'glass. Sempy.	I'm afraid my glass needs refilling.

Sarry, maffit.	No, thank you very much (on being offered a drink).
Liarintilit.	Drink up.
Anor haffun and I'm away w' the Bann.	I'm afraid I have had my quota.
That fella's not only futless he's legless forby.	That chap looks a shade under the weather.
Anor glass and I'll be plastered till the gills.	One more and I'll be quite intoxicated.
Know this? A'm nicely.	I have had sufficient, thank you.
Iffa hev any more I'll be as fulasa po.	I must stop or I'll be properly under the weather.
That boy cudden bite his thum.	That chap over there is in a bad way.

At the Post Office

Wud ye givvus a leff haun stamp?	Could I have an air mail stamp?
The stamp fell on me.	The stamp slipped through my fingers.
Sterrable what postitch costs ye ni.	Postage costs have become extremely expensive.

At the Newsagent's

Haveyea Mirr?	Do you have the *Daily Mirror?*
A'm bianamale.	I would like the *Daily Mail.*
Sixin?	Have you a Sixth Edition of the *Belfast Telegraph?*
Parshal in yit?	Has the *Impartial Reporter* arrived?
Gat the Server?	I would like the *Observer,* please.
Irsh Noose in?	Have you the *Irish News?*
New Sletterin?	Is the *News Letter* in?

In a Shoe Shop

I take sixes but I find sevens so comfortable I wear nines.	Where size is concerned I'm not really sure what fits me.
Last perr I gat here a hedda wear them for a week afore a cud put them on.	I had trouble with the last pair of shoes I bought here.
A'm luckin a perra mutton dummies.	I would like a pair of plimsolls.
I'd like a perra shoes but nat fer wearin.	I am looking for a pair of shoes for formal occasions.
The wee lad's wantin anor perra boots.	I would like a pair of shoes for the boy.

At the Corner Shop

Givvus apounna sassitches.	I would like some pork sausages.
Abaxa chawklets.	Could I have a box of chocolates?
Packitapees.	I would like a packet of peas.
Pounna shugger.	A pound of sugar.

26

Givvus Ferry Lickwood.	Some *Fairy Liquid*, please.
Any smoke addict?	Do you have smoked haddock?
There's a dinge in this tinna-peas.	This tin of peas is dented.
Sapoun.	The price is £1.

At the Greengrocer's

Buncha scallions.	A half-pound of spring onions.
A charra aliffs.	A jar of olives.
A pounna goosegabs.	A pound of gooseberries.
Enny carts?	Have you any carrots?
Sex orranchez.	A half-dozen oranges, please.

ENTERTAINMENT

At the Theatre

Is there a chance affa rosiner at haff-time?

Is there time for a drink during the interval?

Themmuns is useless.

The cast is not terribly impressive.

Hev ye seen this lat makin ijits of themselves before?

Have you seen these players perform before?

That wee thing can't haff act.

The girl in the principal role seems quite talented.

At the Cinema

Any idea wire thissus an ex-pitcher?	Do you happen to know if this is an 'X' certificate film?
Wat's th' big pitcher?	Do you know what is top of the programme?
Yew seen it twyst?	Have you already seen the main attraction?
Sawrite fer th' wanes, issit?	Is the film suitable for children?

At a Party

Yew wunna them?	What religious persuasion are you?
Yer wishes granite.	Your wish is granted.
He's a grate man for the veal.	He's very dedicated, I gather. Always goes to the field for 'the Twelfth'.
Fonda willicks?	Do you like whelks?
Ye cudden bate track ruel.	I am in favour of direct rule.
He goes roun inna hunch-beck.	He drives a smart hatch-back car.
Swayafter twelve. Stime we leff.	It has got rather late.
Shizza plite wee wumman.	The lady seems to be extremely well spoken.
A ast her iffa cud liff her but she said for till ast the cis-ternlaw fer she was swaiten.	I asked her if she would like to dance. She said she was rather warm, but that her sister-in-law might care to.
That fella's leppin about like a hernonna griddle.	He dances with considerable agility.
A think we'll wennar way home.	I feel we should call it a day.

He was that boorn a cud hardly keep miseopen.

I found the gentleman somewhat boring.

John Pepper tickles me in bed every Saturday night.

I enjoy reading John Pepper's column in bed.

I split my sides at something John Pepper wrote in my bath.

I was reading John Pepper while having a bath, and found it most amusing.

My oul man puts neara pounnashugger innis tay, so he dus.

My husband puts an enormous amount of sugar in his tea.

A know ritely them battles flaff th' bekavalarry.

I have a suspicion they didn't come by that wine honestly.

When he has the drink onnim he's violin.

After a few drinks he tends to turn rather violent.

She goes allava dirr when she runs intil him.

When she meets him she seems to lose all self-control.

He keeps goin hirr an yon.

He is very restless.

He's nire one thing nor thorr.

It is difficult to assess his character.

Yer hevvin me awn.

You are pulling my leg.

Her man's ferry chalice.

Her husband is extremely jealous.

Thatwunas haughs likka churn.

The lady who has just left has a pretty sturdy pair of legs.

Dussen marr a bit.

It is quite immaterial.

At a Wedding

They went till th' waddin on their feet.

They decided to walk to the church.

Ye cud see he wus still suffern from his oul leg.

The bridegroom had a distinct limp.

That fella axas iffe wus in the peeritch.

The bridegroom carries himself well.

They're just doatin, th' perra them.

They seem to be very much in love.

He's gat awful corpulin. Ye cud say he's stikkin out.

The bridegroom could do with a little less weight.

Heeesa Pradessan an sheesa Cathalick.	I gather it is a mixed marriage.

In Court

He wussin playin close.	The police officer was not in uniform.
Sleegle.	It is not contrary to the law of the land.
Heesma bannister.	He is my legal representative.
Shees luckin pale.	She is seeking release on her own recognisance.
Hees gataff.	He was found not guilty and discharged.
Heesgat six. Diabalical.	Unfortunately he was found guilty and given a six month sentence.

At a Funeral

This where the dead man lives?	Is this the residence of the deceased?
The corpse's bror wants to know wattar ye hevin?	The brother of the deceased wonders if you would care for a drink.
Wud ye fancy a lift?	Would you like to be one of the pallbearers?
Whatever he died of it doesn't seem to have been anything serious.	The cause of death does not appear to have been due to complications.

At a Football Match

See that reff. Sed's cut.

The referee has a poor idea of the rules of the game.

Reff san ijit. Slostis bap.

The refereeing is quite disastrous.

Thon striker's futless.

The striker hasn't really shown a great degree of skill.

Arwansis fan-tastick.

Our team is playing some good football.

Themmuns can't play fer champ.

The other side's a poor lot.

Arwans shud get stuffed.	The home side just can't do anything right.
See that striker? Stynamite.	The striker has tremendous power.
A cud do better wi' no arms than that nit atween th' posts.	The goalkeeper is of little consequence.
Them bexis useless.	The backs are not terribly impressive.

At a Rugby Match

Yon lad plase wi' thead.	He is an intelligent player.
The full back can kick ritely.	The full back is marvellous.
That boyo's trapple croun material.	The hooker plays exceptionally well.
Gawd but yer man's futwork skrate.	His accuracy as a kicker is quite remarkable.
Why doan the forwards get stuck in?	It is time the forwards showed some enthusiasm.

At the Golf Club

Worst hole on the coorse is the fith.	The fifth hole is extremely difficult.
Ye hafta haunit till him wennies puttin.	He putts very well indeed.
Swood play's stikkin out.	He has a tremendous drive.
He's outa this world wi' a thee iron.	The man plays the three iron with great competence.

At the Doctor's

Cudye get rid af this leg av mine?	I'm having considerable bother with my leg.
Ave gat this thote for thee weeks.	My throat has been painful for nearly a month.
Cud ye banditch my haun?	I would like my wrist bandaged.
Awanta git riddaf mowl stummick.	I have had fairly severe stomach pains.
Cud ye givvus anything to bring my leg to a head?	Could you give me something for my leg?

A hadda walk on m'man's arm or a wudden be here.	I would not have been able to get here without my husband's assistance.
M'man's sister's preggnan agin. Make ye spit.	Me sister-in-law is pregnant again.
Shees vines.	She is suffering from varicose veins.
Mart's awful bad.	I have a worrying pain round my heart.
Ave been bad fer neer a month.	I haven't been feeling well for some weeks.
I fell intil a sheugh and there's thorns in me yit.	I fell into a ditch and I still have thorns I cannot get rid of.
Cud a get meers singed?	I am being bothered by wax in my ears. Can I have them syringed?
Marm sproke.	My arm has been fractured.

At the Chemist's

Ma thums thobbin. Cud ye givvus somethin till stick on-nit.	My thumb is giving me a lot of trouble. A bandage might help it.
Awant catton wool for meers.	Could I have some cotton wool for my ears?
Awanta get ridda ma chest.	Have you a quick-working remedy for a chest complaint?
Mowl hed's splittin.	I have a severe headache.
I hevva bittava hursel.	I have gone hoarse.
Med's been onanaff all day.	I have a headache that keeps coming and going.
Hev ye a cure for information?	Could I have something for a slight inflammation?
Ava brust ulster.	I have an ulcer and I fear it has burst.

Malugs is bored so they are.	I have had my ears pierced.
Givvus a battle ferra caff.	Have you something to ease a bad cough?
A can't heer meers.	I am suffering from a slight deafness.

At the Chiropodist's

My feet's killin me.	I have walked so much that I feel quite exhausted.
You can see the pain of my bunions on my face.	I have done such a lot of walking I really need a rest.
I futted it ivvery fut aff the way.	I did not bother taking a taxi.
My wife won't be at herself till she gets her legs back.	My wife is quite worn out.
I'm aff till the chirapadist about my ingroan toe nail.	I intend to see a chiropodist about this ingrowing toe nail.
A've walked that much the ballsa ma legs is near round the front.	I am quite weary trudging round the shops.
Its that warm ma fettare like baps.	This heat has given me swollen feet.
Them patient shoos made a rite haun affma feet.	I bought a pair of patient shoes and found them most uncomfortable.

There are a number of people the visitor will never actually meet but who often stray into the conversation. It is useful to note their names, and the contexts in which they are mentioned.

Arthur Eyetis	'She has terrible arthritis.'
Billy Stain	Billy has decided not to go home.
Bridget Loan	Available at most banks.
Charlie Sin	Charlie is at home.
Gloria Site	The house has a glorious site.
Harry Soar	Harry is very annoyed.

Ivor Wun	'I for one think it is wrong.'
Mayne Yew	'Me and you both.'
Jimmy Sawn	'Jimmy's on the TV tonight.'
Ken Seer	Ken has arrived.
Maggie Sout	'Maggie isn't in.'
Nora Mean	'Know what I mean?'
Herr Tell	'I have heard.'
Jerry Spack	Jerry has returned.

Relations

Mant Nelly's a rerr tern.	I have an aunt who is quite a character.
He's the spitten image av his bror.	He is remarkably like his brother in appearance.
Kent stan th' brornlaw.	I don't get on terribly well with my brother-in-law.
The childer all take after their da. Take everything they ken lay their hauns on.	In appearance the children tend to resemble their father.
The dornlaw's nisan plite.	Our daughter-in-law is very pleasant.
Slikees farr. A ded loss.	He is rather like his father.
The farnlaw's natta bad sort.	My father-in-law is very likeable.
Ye'd think her grammar yud know better than to put gin intil her hat watter battle.	Her grandmother is full of surprises.
He's onny a haffbror.	I think he's a half-brother.
Her own mornlaw nivver shuts her bake.	Her mother-in-law is somewhat loquacious.
Th' owl man'll be here after.	My husband will be along soon.

If the owlwuman sed she wus cummin she'll be cummin.	My wife will be here directly.
Take thunkell. Spittava laff, so he is.	My uncle is good company.

Christian Names

Alec	**Ellick**
Arthur	**Arter**
Bertie	**Barty**
Billy	**Bully**
Davy	**Tavey**
Dorothy	**Darthy**
Georgie	**Jordy**
Hughie	**Shuey**
Madge	**Match**
Peter	**Peer**
Richard	**Rigid**
Robert	**Rabbit**
Willie	**Wully**
Willie John	**Wully Jawn**

Surnames

Ulster variations of common surnames are full of pitfalls. In this list the normal spelling is given first.

Bennett	**Bent**
Cahoon	**Coon**
Clarke	**Clerk**
Connolly	**Cannaly**
Crymble	**Crimmil**
Curran	**Corn**

Doherty	**Darty**
Donnelly	**Danly**
Douglas	**Tuglass**
Duke	**Chuke**
Falloon	**Floon**
Farren	**Farn**
Faughan	**Fawn**
Field	**Feel**
Gallaher	**Galliker**
Gamble	**Gemmel**
Gillespie	**Glespey**
Haughey	**Hawkeye**
Hewitt	**Shooit**
Lenaghan	**Lenniken**
McCullough	**McCullick**
Morrow	**Mara**
Robinson	**Rabison**
Stephenson	**Stevasin**
Thompson	**Tomsin**
Urquhart	**Urkart**
Vernon	**Vern**
Weatherup	**Wireup**
Wilkinson	**Wilkisen**

Trades and PROFESSIONS

He's a born accountinant. He's grate at the figures.

He is an accountant.

Her a nacktress! Don't make me spit.

She is an actress, really?

He's no more a nectar than mowl granny.

He is surely not an actor.

Ar binmen wud waken the dead.

The binmen here are very noisy.

I leff a note for the braidman to lave four snowtaps an' a corn square.

I have left a note for the baker.

The wee lad lucked like a chibbley cleaner.	The young boy appeared to be a chimney sweep.
She ses she wantsa be a simple serpent.	She has ambitions to be a civil servant.
I sed she shud see a dentiss about her big mouth.	I told her she should see a dentist.
The paper put it in wrong. I'm goin till see the additer.	I intend to complain to the editor.
The lectrishan nivver came till fix th' tally.	The electrician did not repair the television.
Ar garner shudda been a plummer.	Our gardener is impossible.
He's the kine av pummlickan that shud be put behine bars.	As a publican, he runs a very poor establishment.
She's set her wee hart on bein a seeketarry.	The girl wants to become a secretary.
He earns good money for he's a fanman.	He drives a van and does very well for himself.
Ye wudden think the man was a narkiteck.	I did not know he was an architect.

The Time and the WEATHER

It is a common experience in Ulster, whether or not you are a stranger, to be asked for the crack time. This merely means that the questioner wants to be sure that it is as near Greenwich Mean Time as possible, otherwise the inquiry would not be made. It is useful to know how to answer.

Swun.	One o'clock.
Saff wun.	Half-past one.
Stentatoo.	Ten minutes to two.
Stoo.	Two o'clock.
Stenpastoo.	Ten minutes past two.

Saftoo.	Half-past two.
Thee.	Three o'clock.
Safthee.	Half-past three.
Sate.	Eight o'clock.
Saffate.	Half-past eight.
Snine.	Nine o'clock.
Sten.	Ten o'clock.
Saftenn.	Half-past ten.
Sleven.	Eleven o'clock.

The Weather

A reference to the weather is often used as a friendly greeting on a country road, to the confusion of the stranger, and it is useful to understand what the greeting really means.

Swarmwun.	It is rather a warm day.
Bravewun.	Weather conditions could be much worse.
Freesye.	That is an extremely bitter morning.
Skettinwurse.	The weather shows no signs of improving.
Sotsotis.	The weather is very warm.
Spoorwan.	Not much of a day, really.
Sardywun.	That is quite a sharp morning.
Spittinagayon.	It has started to rain.
Steeminagayon.	It has turned showery.
Scowl.	I am really feeling the cold.
Simprovin.	Weather conditions are getting better.
Warmwire.	That is a sultry sort of afternoon.

Shirey.	It looks as if there'll be showers.
Sweat.	It's raining again.
Skettinberr.	It is an improvement on yesterday.
Skeepinup.	The weather seems to be holding.
Splowy.	Isn't it stormy?
Swinnery.	That is a wintry kind of morning.
Swindy.	There is a stong breeze.
Thettinin.	It looks like rain.
Manbut thate's chranic.	My goodness but that's a terribly hot day.

Agriculture is an important part of the Ulster economy, and to a greater extent than in many other areas weather conditions are a persistent subject of comment.

Gran fer th' raipin.	The conditions are excellent for the harvest.
Mans is all japped.	My hands are chapped with the cold.
It was that cowl last night a near gat my enn.	The glass fell sharply last night.
That day wud founner ye.	My goodness but it is bitterly cold.
Hevven seen suchana wile night ferages.	The weather was as bad last night as I have experienced for a long time.
Agat caught inna shire anam ringin.	I was unlucky enough to be caught in the rain.
Stamp kine affa day.	Looks like we're in for more rain.
Stry for this timaff the year.	It has turned out dry.
Wire's gat nissen mile.	The day has turned out pleasantly mild.

49

Numbers and COLOURS

Numbers

Wan (in some areas **yin**)	One
Do	Two
Thee (in some areas **free**)	Three
Fower	Four
Fiave	Five
Sax (in some areas **sex**)	Six

Savin	Seven
Eyate	Eight
Nian	Nine
Tenn	Ten
Levan	Eleven

Colours

Vilet	Violet
Yella	Yellow
Browan	Brown
Orenje	Orange
Bludshat	Red
Cray	Grey
Wyte	White
Plew	Blue

Survival KITS

Many phrases are spoken almost exclusively in particular cities, towns and regions of the Province. The following is a sample of what you may come across in Belfast, Ballymena, and Ards.

Belfast Survival Kit

Farras a'm concerned saw-laff.

I am afraid the deal is off.

Ware's th' war works?

Could you direct me to the 'Water Works', please?

Sneer nine.

It is almost nine o'clock.

Spout seven.	It is about seven o'clock.
Mopen toffers.	I am open to offers.
A've a bror in Tranna.	I have a brother living in Toronto.
Monday was a fortnight when it happened.	It happened two weeks ago last Monday.
Sheese rite surt. Give me a glassawatter inna cup.	The lady very kindly gave me a drink of water.
A redd out ma stummick tiller.	I spoke my mind to her.
Sonny a wee plout.	It is only a light shower.
Know watta mane?	Do you understand what I'm trying to say?
She scrubbed her guts out.	As a cleaner she worked very hard.
Eesa cappen in tharmy.	He has the rank of captain in one of the top regiments.
Pity affim. He's dundan.	Unfortunately he has been made redundant.
Stussen maer.	It is quite immaterial.
Middasajeg.	My father drives a Jaguar car.

Ballymena Survival Kit

Ballymena is one area where the accent produces variations so considerable that a sharp ear and a degree of local knowledge are essential.

A dinna ken him frae Adam.	I do not know the gentleman.
He let onnis feet.	He certainly landed well.
He's that mane he wudden gie ye the time o day.	He is inordinately parsimonious.
A clapped een onner onny thorra day.	I saw her only recently.
A'd rarr hev him nor her.	I prefer him to his wife.

Shizza girn.	She is continually complaining.
He was on the groon, fu.	He was lying on his back.
He hut ar wee dug waya stane.	He threw a stone at our dog.
Shiz onny an owl girn.	She is extremely talkative.
A saw her abin th' cassey.	I saw her just past the forecourt.
We hev wer tay at sex.	We usually have tea around six o'clock.
Her beg wus stuffed till the gills way rubbitch.	Her handbag was absolutely crammed.
The tay's on the bile.	The tea is ready.
Givver a bowel av parritch an' she's on th' pig's beck.	She is very fond of a bowl of porridge.
He cannae dae a haun's turn ivver since he fell intil a sheugh.	He is still suffering from the time he fell into a ditch.
He cannae coont for champ.	His arithmetic is fairly indifferent.
A wus ferr deeved by the noise.	The sound deafened me.
The aul clauk disnae tell the reet time.	The clock does not appear to be quite accurate.
He's shoon wur all clabber.	His shoes were in a dreadful state.
The shap wus thrang.	The store was crowded with shoppers.
He wrot in the feels all his born days.	He has been a farmer all his life.
She giv the wee thing a quare skelp.	She hit the child a rather severe blow.

Ards Survival Kit

A canny dae.	I can do nothing about it.
A brung it hame under me oxter.	I carried it home under my arm.

Boat's just abin the harber. Way her heid's doon she must be haven a hunderd cran.	Our boat is about to dock. She looks as if she has at least one hundred cran of herring.
Wunna these days a'm ginnae show thon dug ma boot.	I intend to do something about their dog shortly.

In a Catastrophe

Expressions of astonishment with which to greet news of a catastrophe are well defined. Any one of the following can appropriately be used in response to any of the statements quoted, and they are freely interchangeable.

My wife has run off with the lodger.	**Yer jokin.**
Our house was burned to the ground last night.	**Awayor that.**
I've lost every penny of my redundancy money on the dogs.	**Ye don't say.**
A burgler took every penny we had when we were away on holiday.	**For goodness sake.**
The wife's having twins.	**Away to hell.**
The boy broke a leg playing rugby.	**Suffern duck.**
The wife crashed the car and it's a write-off.	**Nivver heard the like.**
I've lost my driving licence for a year.	**Cheese.**

Dialogues
TRANSLATED

In a Bar

This customer is engaged in the process of ordering a vodka and white lemonade.

'**Vodkan wyte.**'
'Pardon?'

'**Vodkan wyte.**'
'Vodka and what?'

'**No, vodkan wyte.**'
'Oh, white? White what?'

'**Wyte lemolade.**'
'What do you mean, white lemonade? It's the only colour we have.'

'**Wumman, dear there's broun.**'
'Broun?'

'**That's right. Broun.**'
'But what on earth's broun?'

'**Broun. Y'know, the colour av Scotch.**'

In a Chippy

This customer orders fish and chips, but is told that fish is not available, nor are pies, although there are small Cornish pasties. He settles for a pasty with peas and vinegar, and goes out into the cold night.

'Fashupper.'

'Fashisaff.'

'Pysupper, then.'

'Pysesafftoo.'

'Pastiesthen?'

'Onnyweans.'

'Pastysupperthen. Annacartanapeas.'

'Vinnikeronyerpeas?'

'Aye, vinniker.'

'Scowlnite.'

'Scowlallrite.'

In a Bus

This speaker is telling a friend that he has stopped drinking and smoking during Lent.

'Maffit.'

'Affwat?'

'Aff thadrink.'

'Yarnat.'

'Maffthafegstoo.'

'Yamaneyer own?'

'Ivverybody's.'

'Sins wen?'

'Sins Sardy.'

'Fer wi?'

'Slent.'

'Ritenuf, affergat.'

In a Supermarket

Someone is suggesting to a friend that they might meet on Sunday. This does not suit. Tuesday is proposed but this is also unsuitable, and Thursday is suggested. Finally, Saturday is proposed, accepted and the arrangement is confirmed.

'Seeyasundi?'

'Naw, Chewsdi?'

'Thirsty mebbe?'

'Naw, Sardy?'

'Sardildo.'

'Riteyar.'

Test Your Word POWER

A simple way to test your word power is to cover up the right-hand column before checking your interpretation with the first column.

Binafleg?	Would you like to purchase a flag?
Watsit nadeaff?	What is the appeal on behalf of?
Luckatis dile.	The gentleman's face is a sight.
Heerweerstain.	We are determined to remain here.
Sannowl sayin.	It is an old proverb.
Youse plain?	Are you playing?
Senaffa nearer.	It is the end of an era.
Dozen marr.	It doesn't matter in the least.
Awanta vintitch whine.	I prefer a good wine.
He made a right hannaf ma fut.	He hurt my foot severely.
He wonna sheel at the baxin.	He is the holder of a shield for boxing.
He can sing noan.	As a vocalist he is not particularly accomplished.
Seeinasyermacusin . . .	In view of the fact that you are my cousin . . .
Seeinasyeastme . . .	In view of the fact that you were good enough to invite me along . . .
Seeinasyerafren . . .	Taking into consideration the fact that you are an old acquaintance . . .

Seeinasyerwunnafuss . . .   Having regard to the fact that we share the same religious beliefs . . .

Shillitonnerfeet.   She was left a handsome legacy.

A Morr Tung
QUIZ

Answer the questions in this Morr Tung *fun quiz and see if you think the pitfalls of Ulster's lively vernacular would hold no terrors for you.*

1. You are at a party and someone seeking your advice draws you aside and says, 'I haven't been'. What do you say?

   (a) 'Where?'

   (b) 'Why, did you miss the bus?'

   (c) 'Do you hope to, eventually?'

2. A woman sitting beside you on a bus says conversationally, 'I bought the chile a scribblin jarr'. What is your comment?

   (a) 'That's an expensive toy, is it not?'

   (b) 'Has he a sweet tooth?'

   (c) 'I presume he has a literary bent, then?'

3. You are standing in a shopping queue and a woman beside you says, 'The boy has a bittava sturr'. How do you react?

   (a) 'Has he defective vision?'

   (b) 'He should see a doctor.'

   (c) 'He should soon get over that.'

4. A woman to whom you have just been introduced says, 'See m'man? Styin about roas munn' How do you comment?

   (a) 'He must have a good appetite.'

   (b) 'Obviously he likes your cooking.'

   (c) 'I have a weakness for it myself.'

5. You arrive at the home of your prospective host and are asked, 'Are you after your dinner?' What do you say?

   (a) 'Thank you, I have already dined.'

(b) 'I'm not expecting it.'

(c) 'Is this an invitation to a meal?'

6. You are a guest at a party and one of the people you meet informs you, 'He's styin about samman'. What reply do you make?

(a) 'Oh, then he's staying for some days.'

(b) 'He is observing a Jewish festival, is he?'

(c) 'Obviously he is extremely fond of salmon.'

7. You overhear a woman telling a friend, 'A brungerup masell'. How would you respond if this information had been addressed to you?

(a) 'Did you indeed?'

(b) 'You surprise me.'

(c) 'You deserve every credit.'

8. A woman beside you in the train sees it is raining and exclaims, 'It's wet and my back's fullaf washin'. What do you say to her?

(a) 'That's too bad.'

(b) 'The train had better not be late, then.'

(c) 'You obviously have a delicate back.'

9. While walking in the park a stranger, taking you to be the owner of a stray dog, says to you, 'If that dog doesn't behave I'll show it my boot'. What form does your reply take?

(a) 'I don't think it would know much about footwear.'

(b) 'Why, do you wear Hush Puppies?'

(c) 'Are you out to teach it a lesson?'

Check your Score

1. a, 0; b, 0; c, 3.   *2. a, 0; b, 0; c, 3.*   *3. a, 0; b, 3; c, 2.*
4. a, 3; b, 2; c, 1.   *5. a, 3; b, 0; c, 0.*   *6. a, 0; b, 0; c, 3.*
7. a, 0; b, 0; c, 3.   *8. a, 3; b, 3; c, 0.*   *9. a, 0; b, 0; c, 3.*

If you scored 0-9: Be prepared for suspicious looks; 10-17: You will be labelled a stranger; 18-24: You will nearly get by, but not quite; 25 and above: You will survive with flying colours.

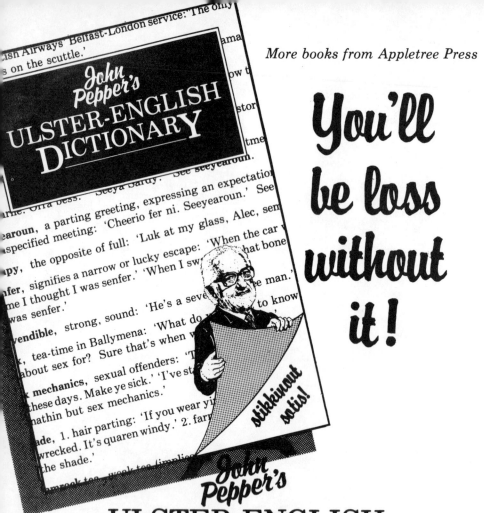

'What a wonderful talent John Pepper is! Over the years we have become familiar with Mr Pepper's recording of Ulster speech, but now Mr Pepper has come up with his best book yet.'

—Newtownards Chronicle

'John Pepper could make up a story out of the weather forecast. He is a man who has a way with words which he uses as a craftsman uses his tools. His writing flows like a placid stream.'

—Ireland's Saturday Night

'I don't advise reading John Pepper among a crowd of strangers or they'll probably think you're daft when you do as I did and start laughing aloud.'

—Ulster Star

'John Pepper does with the printed word what the late great James Young did with the spoken word.'

—News Letter

'Even if you were not born in the North there are a few hundred laughs to be had from it. What the average Belfast-man does to the English language isn't ordinary and what makes it all even more incredible is that what he does to it is almost always funny.'

—Irish Times

'John Pepper is to be congratulated on the way in which he has brought together the best of the wealth of material at his disposal.'

—Irish Weekly

'There are a hundred laughs to be got out of John Pepper's **Ulster-English Dictionary.**'

—Sunday Press

'John Pepper . . . made me laugh till the tears rolled down my cheeks.'

—Farmweek

MY LADY OF THE CHIMNEY CORNER/ THE SOULS OF POOR FOLK.
Alexander Irvine

'This publication is most welcome, for anyone who owns an earlier edition is most unlikely to lend it and the time is ripe for another generation of readers to be introduced to one of Ulster's greatest literary sons, not merely because he finally achieved greatness, but because of the warm humanity of his writings. Together 'My Lady' and 'The Souls', are now established as masterpieces of contemporary literature'
—Norman Ballantine, *Belfast News Letter*

FACES OF THE PAST
Brian Mercer Walker

'By combining both photographic and literary material and concentrating on poems and prose by local writers, he (Brian Walker) hopes to show something of what it was like to be alive between 1880 and 1915 . . . and the idea had worked in a very haunting way . . . the pictures and words in *Faces of the Past* seem to evoke a poignant, lost world'
—Suzanne Lowry *The Guardian*

'. . . an old woman eating her spuds and washing them down with buttermilk in the harvest-field; a temperance reformer badgering people in the pubs . . . the book is an excellent introduction to the mind of Ulster, as well as a wide window opening out on the past'
—Benedict Kiely *Irish Times*

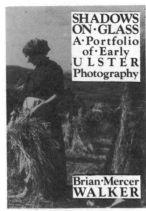

SHADOWS ON GLASS
Brian Mercer Walker

'A fascinating book showing various aspects of Ulster life, rural and urban, high and low, between the 1860s and 1920s ... Mary Young's pictures show the life of the well-heeled huntin', fishin' and shootin' class. At the other end of the spectrum are Rose Shaw's pictures, which reproduce the life of the farm labourers of the Clogher Valley with a sympathy as near to poetry as makes no difference.'
—Bryan MacMahon in *The Irish Times*

Brian Mercer Walker's celebrated study of the life and times of thirteen early photographers in Ulster presents over 100 photographs, most of them published here for the first time. While some are from well-known collections, many have only come to light in the past few years and as Brian Walker writes in his introduction: 'Brief moments of light and shade captured by the photographer on fragile, plate glass negatives, these photographs present us today with strong and lasting images of a lost world.'

EDWARDIAN BELFAST A Social Profile
Sybil Gribbon

Edwardian Belfast is a fresh and lively investigation of social conditions and mores in Belfast at the turn of the century, based on official records, newspapers and reminiscences. Together with over twenty remarkable and hitherto unpublished photographs by the Belfast photographer, Alex R Hogg, this fascinating portrait will arouse new interest in life in the northern capital on the eve of the Ulster Crisis and the outbreak of the First World War.

TURN UP THE LAMP   J. S. Doran
Tales of a Mourne Childhood

J. S. Doran grew up in the early 1900s in Kilkeel, a market town and fishing port situated between the Mournes and the Co. Down coast. *Turn Up the Lamp* is his account of the people, places and events which impinged upon a particularly observed child: country people and fair days, fishermen and their craft, and travelling people and players are among the subjects portrayed here with the innocence and sensuality of childhood.

'He writes in a style reminiscent of his native Mourne granite—strong and without frills . . . and one could not find a better guide to them (the Mournes) than Doran'

—Books Ireland

TRAVELLER IN THE GLENS   Jack McBride

As Jack McBride points out in his introduction, the Glens of Antrim have achieved fame by just being themselves. Besides customs and beliefs peculiar to its people, this tour of the region includes accounts of its crafts and craftsmen, dialect and verse, well-known people and characters, and many other aspects of life which combine to give the area its unique atmosphere.

THE DAY
THE MONSTER CAME
John Gray

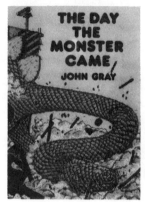

A freak storm in the Irish Sea awakens a huge troglodite, dormant for thousands of years. Its emergence in Ballymacarrett threatens the entire area, and after violent attempts by adult forces to counter the threat, which merely aggravate the monster, it remains for the children of the district to try to find a solution. Their efforts will enthrall children everywhere.

THERE ARE DRAGONS
John Gray

Michael is a lonely Belfast boy who dreams of having a pet, but his fussy, pestering mother won't permit it. And then, one day, a visit to Boxy, the old man at the corner shop marks the beginning of a strange and wonderful adventure . . . For eight-to-eleven year-olds. 'Refreshing to see a children's book that relates in locality and jargon directly to the readers . . . a wee gem . . . This author is improving all the time'—*Belfast News Letter*